# ENDANGERED ELEPHANTS

**Bobbie Kalman**

🌳 **Crabtree Publishing Company**

www.crabtreebooks.com

# Earth's Endangered Animals Series
## A Bobbie Kalman Book

Dedicated by Patti Loesche
To the elephants of Lake Manyara National Park, Tanzania,
and the people who protect them.

**Author and Editor-in-Chief**
Bobbie Kalman

**Substantive editor**
Kathryn Smithyman

**Project editor**
Kristina Lundblad

**Editors**
Molly Aloian
Robin Johnson
Kelley MacAulay
Niki Walker

**Research**
Laura Hysert

**Design**
Margaret Amy Reiach

**Cover design and series logo**
Samantha Crabtree

**Production coordinator**
Katherine Kantor

**Photo research**
Crystal Foxton

**Consultant**
Patricia Loesche, Ph.D., Animal Behavior Program,
Department of Psychology, University of Washington

**Illustrations**
Barbara Bedell: page 5
Katherine Kantor: pages 7 (bottom left), 13, 27
Bonna Rouse: page 7 (top and bottom right)

**Photographs**
Bruce Coleman Inc.: Stuart L. Craig Jr.: page 25
Dave Ferris - AEACP, 2003, www.elephantart.com: page 30
James Lemass/Index Stock: page 27
Minden Pictures: Gerry Ellis: page 29 (top);
   Frans Lanting: page 19 (bottom), 23, 28;
   Claus Meyer: page 29 (bottom);
   Konrad Wothe: page 24
Naturepl.com: Torsten Brehm: page 20
Photo Researchers Inc.: Art Wolfe: page 14;
   John Reader: page 22
Other images by Corel, Digital Stock, and Digital Vision

## Crabtree Publishing Company

www.crabtreebooks.com    1-800-387-7650

Copyright © **2005 CRABTREE PUBLISHING COMPANY**.
All rights reserved. No part of this publication may be
reproduced, stored in a retrieval system or be transmitted in
any form or by any means, electronic, mechanical, photocopying,
recording, or otherwise, without the prior written permission
of Crabtree Publishing Company. In Canada: We acknowledge the
financial support of the Government of Canada through the Book
Publishing Industry Development Program (BPIDP) for our
publishing activities.

Cataloging-in-Publication Data
Kalman, Bobbie.
  Endangered elephants / Bobbie Kalman.
    p. cm. -- (Earth's endangered animals series)
  Includes index.
  ISBN-13: 978-0-7787-1860-4 (RLB)
  ISBN-10: 0-7787-1860-3 (RLB)
  ISBN-13: 978-0-7787-1906-9 (pbk.)
  ISBN-10: 0-7787-1906-5 (pbk.)
  1. Elephants-Juvenile literature. 2. Endangered species-Juvenile
literature. I. Title.
  QL737.P98K36 2005
  599.67'168--dc22
                       2005000349
                           LC

**Published in
the United States**
PMB16A
350 Fifth Ave.
Suite 3308
New York, NY
10118

**Published
in Canada**
616 Welland Ave.,
St. Catharines, Ontario
Canada
L2M 5V6

**Published in the
United Kingdom**
73 Lime Walk
Headington
Oxford
OX3 7AD
United Kingdom

**Published
in Australia**
386 Mt. Alexander Rd.,
Ascot Vale (Melbourne)
VIC 3032

# Contents

Endangered! 4

What are elephants? 6

Where do elephants live? 8

Elephant bodies 10

From calf to adult 12

Elephant herds 14

Elephant behavior 16

Elephant food 18

Habitat loss 20

Ivory poaching 22

Working elephants 24

Safe places for elephants 26

People helping elephants 28

Create elephant art! 30

Glossary and Index 32

# Endangered!

Elephants are **endangered** animals. Fewer than one hundred years ago, millions of elephants lived on Earth. Today, there are only about a half million elephants left. If people do not work to protect elephants, these animals may soon become **extinct**.

## Words to know

Scientists use certain words to describe animals that are in danger. Some of these words are listed below.

**vulnerable** Describes animals that may become endangered because they face dangers in the **wild**

**endangered** Describes animals that are in danger of dying out in the wild

**critically endangered** Describes animals that are at high risk of dying out in the wild

**extinct** Describes animals that have died out or that have not been seen in the wild for at least 50 years

# What are elephants?

Elephants are **mammals**. Mammals are **warm-blooded** animals. The bodies of warm-blooded animals stay about the same temperature no matter how hot or cold their surroundings are. All mammals have **backbones**, and most have hair or fur on their bodies. Baby mammals drink milk from the bodies of their mothers.

## Like no other

Elephants belong to the *Elephantidae* family. They are the only type of animal in this family. Elephants are huge animals that have big ears, long trunks, and **tusks**. Tusks are long pointed teeth.

*Elephants are sometimes called **pachyderms**. Pachyderm means "thick-skinned."*

## Three of a kind

There are three kinds of elephants—Asian elephants, African **savanna** elephants, and African forest elephants. Elephants live in some of the hottest places on Earth. Asian elephants live in parts of Asia, including India, Thailand, and China. African savanna elephants live in Africa, south of the Sahara desert. African forest elephants live in the central and western parts of Africa.

*Asian elephants rarely have tusks, and their ears are smaller than the ears of other kinds of elephants.*

*African forest elephants are the smallest kind of elephants. They have long pink tusks.*

*African savanna elephants are the largest kind of elephants. They have long white tusks.*

7

# Where do elephants live?

Different elephants live in different **habitats**. A habitat is the natural place where an animal lives. Some elephants live only in one habitat, such as a forest. Other elephants move among several habitats searching for food.

Asian elephants and African forest elephants live mainly in **rain forests**. African savanna elephants, such as the one shown below, live mainly on dry grasslands. These elephants also travel to mountains, deserts, forests, and swamps.

*Elephants live in places with plenty of food and water.*

8

*Elephants visit several **water holes** each day. They drink the water. They also swim and take baths in the water. The Asian elephant, shown above, is taking a bath.*

# Elephant bodies

Elephants are the largest land animals on Earth. Elephants grow throughout their entire lives, so the biggest elephants are also the oldest elephants. African savanna elephants, such as the one shown here, grow larger than do other kinds of elephants. Male elephants are larger than the female elephants of their kind.

*Elephants have twelve **molars**, or grinding teeth. They use their molars to chew plants.*

*Both kinds of African elephants have tusks that do not stop growing. Tusks are made of **ivory**.*

## The amazing trunk

An elephant's trunk is its upper lip and nose. The elephant uses its trunk to breathe, to smell, and to suck up water. The trunk is **prehensile**. Prehensile means "able to grasp, lift, and throw." All elephants can use their trunks to lift objects that are as heavy as trees. They can also grasp objects as tiny as berries.

Elephants flap their large ears to keep their bodies cool.

Elephants have tough, thick, and wrinkled skin. The wrinkles trap water, which keeps the elephants cool.

Elephants have long hairs at the ends of their tails. They use their tails to swat insects.

Elephants have thick pads on the bottoms of their feet. The pads help elephants walk without making much noise.

# From calf to adult

Every animal goes through a set of changes from the time it is born to the time it is an adult. This set of changes is called a **life cycle**. An elephant's life cycle begins when it is born. A baby elephant is called a **calf**. A young elephant is called a **juvenile**. When an elephant becomes **mature**, or an adult, it can **mate**, or join together with another elephant to make babies of its own.

*An animal's **life span** is the length of time the animal is alive. An elephant lives for about 70 years.*

# The life cycle of an elephant

Before it is born, a calf grows and develops inside its mother's body for about 22 months. A calf can walk soon after it is born. In its first year, a calf stays close to its mother.

A juvenile depends on its mother until it is mature at about ten years of age. A mature male elephant is called a **bull**. A mature female elephant is called a **cow**.

*A calf is hairy when it is born. It weighs about 250 pounds (113.4 kg). It uses its trunk to smell and to feel its way around.*

*A mature elephant is old enough to mate when it is between ten and thirteen years old.*

*At first, the calf feeds only on milk from its mother's body. After several months, the calf begins eating other foods and drinking water.*

*A juvenile plays a lot! It also learns how to use its trunk to find food. As the juvenile grows, its skin gets thicker. Some juvenile elephants start growing tusks.*

13

# Elephant herds

Most elephants live in family groups called **herds**. A herd is made up of cows and their young. Male elephants leave the herd when they become bulls, but the cows stay with the herd. Some herds have as few as five elephants, whereas others have as many as 50 elephants!

## Raise and protect

Elephants that are in a herd travel, find food, sleep, and bathe together. The cows also help one another raise and protect their calves. If a calf wanders too far from the herd, one of the cows will quickly guide it back with her trunk, as shown left.

## The matriarch

The oldest cow is the leader of the herd. She is called the **matriarch**. The matriarch is very helpful to the herd. She knows where to find food and water. She also leads the herd away from danger.

## Bachelor herds

As male elephants mature, they become violent. The matriarch drives the bulls out of her herd. Some bulls then live alone. Others live in small groups called **bachelor herds**. Bulls visit cows only to mate.

*Bulls fight by shoving one another, wrestling with their trunks, and using their tusks as swords. The bulls above are trunk wrestling.*

# Elephant behavior

Female elephants do everything together, including taking baths. As they bathe, they spray one another with water and play. The elephants then roll in mud or spray mud onto their bodies with their trunks, as shown above. The mud protects their skin from insect bites. It also helps keep the elephants cool.

## Snooze time

Elephants sleep at night and during the hottest times of the day. During the day, they often sleep standing up, with their trunks drooping to the ground or resting on top of their tusks. At night, elephants sleep lying on their sides. They often snore while they sleep!

16

## Elephant talk

Elephants make many sounds to **communicate**, or send messages to one another. They snort, squeal, and **trumpet** with their trunks. They also make low rumbling sounds called **infrasound** to call out to one another over long distances. Infrasound is a sound that is too low for humans to hear.

## Showing affection

Elephants also communicate using their bodies. The cows in a herd show **affection**, or loving feelings, for one another and for their calves. They touch one another gently with their trunks and sometimes rest their heads together. Calves often lean against their mothers to rest or to be comforted.

*Elephants use their trunks to touch one another and also to sniff one another's **scent**, or smell. They wrap their trunks together to say "hello."*

# Elephant food

Elephants spend most of the day **foraging**, or searching for food, and eating. They are **herbivores**. Herbivores are animals that eat mainly plants. Grasses, fruits, twigs, leaves, water plants, and seeds are the main foods that elephants eat.

Elephants eat bark, too. They strip bark from trees using their tusks. They also use their tusks to dig up dirt and rocks at **salt licks**. Salt licks are places where the soil is full of salt.

Elephants must eat salt to stay healthy.

*Each day, an elephant can eat up to 300 pounds (136 kg) of food and drink up to 50 gallons (189 l) of water.*

## A lot of water

Elephants drink a lot of water! They use their long trunks to suck up water and squirt it down their throats. In hot, dry weather, the water in some rivers dries up. When water is hard to find, elephants dig up dry **riverbeds** using their tusks. They dig to find water that is buried deep under ground.

*If elephants stayed in one place for too long, they would soon eat all the plants! A matriarch constantly leads her herd from place to place in search of food and water. Many herds travel to the same places year after year.*

**19**

# Habitat loss

One of the main dangers to elephants is **habitat loss**. Habitat loss is the destruction of the natural places where animals live.

## Clearing the land

The number of people who live in Africa and Asia is growing. Every year, people need more and more space for farms and homes. As towns and cities grow, people often destroy elephant habitats by **clearing**. To clear means to remove all the plants from an area. Many areas that have been cleared were once places where elephants found food.

*People sometimes clear land by setting fire to plants. The fires destroy elephant habitats. Some elephants are also killed by the fires. This Asian elephant is in the path of a fire.*

20

## Not enough food!

When the trees and other plants that elephants usually eat are gone, elephants often eat **crops** grown by farmers. Some hungry elephants even take food from houses and barns! People have been hurt or killed by hungry elephants. Some people get angry at the elephants and kill them using guns and fires. Many elephants are poisoned.

*These elephants have come to a farmer's field in search of food.*

# Ivory poaching

*Elephant poachers killed many elephants to get the tusks shown above.*

It is **illegal**, or against the law, to hunt elephants and other endangered animals, but many people **poach** elephants to take their ivory tusks. To poach means to kill animals illegally. Most poaching occurs in Africa, where the elephants have long tusks. **Poachers** have been killing elephants for their tusks for thousands of years. The ivory is used to make expensive pieces of art and jewelry.

## Hunted down

In the last 50 years, automatic weapons have made it easier for people to kill large numbers of elephants. Poachers often kill entire herds, including calves that do not yet have tusks.

## Killed during wars

Some African countries are at war. Elephants cannot get the food and water they need when armies are fighting in their habitats. Elephant habitats are sometimes completely destroyed by wars. Some armies kill elephants for ivory, then sell the ivory to pay for their weapons.

## No more trade!

In the 1980s, people realized that elephants were becoming endangered because of poaching. Around the world, people were encouraged to stop the **ivory trade**. The ivory trade is the buying and selling of ivory products. Many countries agreed to **ban** ivory trading. Since the ban was put in place, there has been less poaching, and the number of elephants is slowly beginning to grow. Some poachers continue to kill elephants, however.

*These men work to protect elephants by punishing poachers. The poacher they caught had these tusks with him.*

# Working elephants

For thousands of years, people have captured Asian elephants and forced them to work. People use elephants for work because elephants can move heavy objects. The work can be dangerous for elephants. Working elephants are separated from their herds. Few are allowed to return to their habitats. Most work until they die.

## Elephants in logging

In Asia, people capture and train elephants to work in **logging**. Logging is a business in which trees are pulled down so that people can use the wood. People called **mahouts** train elephants to pull down trees and move logs. Some mahouts are cruel to elephants.

*Many Asian countries have banned the use of elephants for logging, but some people still use Asian elephants illegally for logging.*

## Circus animals

People all over the world enjoy watching elephants perform in circuses. Elephants are quick learners and can be trained to do many tricks.

## Dangerous jobs

Performing in circuses can be dangerous for elephants, however. Some trainers beat or starve circus elephants to make them perform. Many places have banned the use of elephants and other animals in circuses.

*Even if they are treated well, circus elephants suffer because they have lost the support and affection of their herds.*

25

# Safe places for elephants

Many countries, including South Africa, are helping elephants in the wild by setting aside areas of land for **preserves**. Preserves are places where animals are protected by a government from poaching and habitat loss. Elephant preserves are usually located where elephants already live.

## Nature corridors

Some governments have set aside strips of land as **corridors**, or paths, between preserves. The corridors are the paths that elephants have always traveled. Elephants use the corridors to move safely from preserve to preserve to get to the water and food that they need.

# Zoo life

If you have seen an elephant, it was likely in a zoo. Many zoos take good care of their elephants and provide them with large areas in which to live. Some zoos have teams of scientists that study elephants. By studying elephants in zoos, scientists learn more about elephants in the wild. Some zoos try to help elephants by giving male and female elephants safe places for mating and having babies.

*These children are learning about elephants by visiting them at a zoo.*

## Living in peace

Some people in Africa and Asia protect their crops and homes from elephants without harming these animals. They build electric fences or dig deep, wide ditches around their lands that elephants cannot cross. People also use bright lights, fires, and drums to scare away the elephants without hurting them.

# People helping elephants

People all over the world work hard to help elephants. Some work for organizations that protect elephants and their habitats. These organizations help elephants by paying for preserves or by passing laws that punish poachers. Other people help elephants by donating money to keep the organizations running.

## Help one, help many

Elephants are a **keystone species**. A keystone species is a group of animals that are especially important in nature. Elephants tear down trees and eat them, allowing smaller plants to grow. The plants that grow are food for many animals. Without elephants, other animals would not have enough plants to eat.

28

## Hope for orphans

Many elephant calves become orphans when the adult elephants in their herd are captured or killed. The calves are left alone. Without older elephants to help them, calves cannot learn how to find food. Some **conservationists** look for orphaned elephant calves. They care for the calves so the calves will not starve.

## Visiting elephants

Visitors to Asia and Africa can help save elephants, too. Some people pay money to see elephants and other animals living in their natural habitats. The money these tourists spend encourages local people to protect elephants. Some people believe, however, that large numbers of tourists damage elephant habitats.

# Create elephant art!

You can help elephants by learning more about them. Share with other people the information you learn about elephants and how they are losing their habitats. One way to teach others about elephants is to have an art show.

You and your friends can draw pictures or make paintings of elephants. Invite your family and friends to your art show, so you can teach them about elephants in danger. Perhaps your art show will inspire someone to help elephants!

## Elephant artists

The Asian Elephant Art and Conservation Project (AEACP) is a group of people who help elephants and mahouts stop working in logging. The AEACP cares for elephants in preserves and gives them safer jobs—as artists! Mahouts teach elephants to grip paintbrushes with their trunks. The elephants then paint pictures with paints that are safe for them to use. The paintings sell for thousands of dollars! The money supports the elephants and their mahouts.

## Learn more!

Learn more about these amazing animals! Visit your local library and search for books to read and videos to watch about elephants. You can also visit these websites:

•**www.himandus.net/elephanteria/index.html**—Have fun learning about elephants through jokes, cartoons, and quizzes.

•**www.nationalgeographic.com/kids**—Click on "Creature Features." Then click on "Elephants, African." You can send an elephant postcard to a friend!

•**http://elephant.elehost.com**—Learn more about how people around the world are helping to save elephants!

# Glossary

**Note**: Boldfaced words that are defined in the text may not appear in the glossary.

**backbone** A row of bones that runs down the middle of an animal's back

**ban** To forbid or not allow someone to do something

**conservationist** A person who works to protect animals and their habitats

**crops** Plants grown by people for food

**infrasound** Sound that cannot be heard by humans but can be felt as vibrations

**ivory** A hard, yellowish white substance that forms the tusks of elephants

**keystone species** A kind of animal or plant on which other animals and plants rely for their survival

**poacher** A person who hunts and kills animals when it is against the law

**prehensile** Able to grasp

**rain forest** A forest found in warm parts of the world that receives over 80 inches (203 cm) of rain each year

**riverbed** The bottom and sides of a river that are usually covered by water

**savanna** A broad, flat grassland found in warm parts of the world

**trumpet** A loud shrill sound made by an elephant, often to express fear or anger

**water hole** A natural pool where water collects and to which animals come to drink and bathe

**wild** The natural places where animals live, which are not protected by people

# Index

Africa 7, 20, 22, 23, 26, 27, 29
African forest elephants 7, 8, 10
African savanna elephants 7, 8, 10
Asia 7, 20, 24, 27, 29
Asian elephants 7, 8, 9, 20, 24
bulls 13, 14, 15
calves 12, 13, 14, 15, 17, 22, 29
communication 17

cows 13, 14, 15, 17
food 8, 13, 14, 15, 18, 19, 20, 21, 23, 26, 28, 29
habitat 8, 20, 23, 24, 28, 29, 30
habitat loss 20, 26
helping elephants 26, 27, 28-29, 30, 31
herds 14-15, 17, 19, 22, 24, 25, 29
ivory 10, 22, 23
life cycle 12-13

matriarchs 15, 19
poaching 22-23, 26, 28
preserves 26, 28, 30
trunks 6, 10, 13, 14, 15, 16, 17, 19, 30
tusks 6, 7, 10, 13, 15, 16, 18, 19, 22, 23
water 8, 9, 10, 11, 13, 15, 16, 18, 19, 23, 26
zoos 27

1 2 3 4 5 6 7 8 9 0  Printed in the U.S.A.  4 3 2 1 0 9 8 7 6 5